Manual
for Intensive
BRIEF
and
EMERGENCY
PSYCHOTHERAPY (B.E.P.)

by

LEOPOLD BELLAK, M.D.

Clinical Professor of Psychiatry
Albert Einstein College of Medicine/
Montefiore Medical Center

Clinical Professor of Psychology
Post-Doctoral Program in Psychotherapy
New York University

Library of Congress Cataloging-in-Publication Data

Bellak, Leopold, 1916—
  Manual for brief and emergency psychotherapy (B.E.P.)

  To be used in conjunction with: Handbook of intensive
brief and emergency psychotherapy (B.E.P.) / by
Leopold Bellak and Helen Siegel.
  Bibliography: p.
  Includes index.
  1. Psychotherapy, Brief—Handbooks, manuals, etc.
2. Psychiatric emergencies—Handbooks, manuals, etc.
I. Bellak, Leopold, 1916—   . Handbook of intensive
brief and emergency psychotherapy (B.E.P.) II. Title.
III. Title: Brief and emergency psychotherapy (B.E.P.)
[DNLM: 1. Crisis Intervention—handbooks. 2. Emergencies
—handbooks. 3. Psychotherapy, Brief—methods—handbooks.

WM 34 B435h 1983 Suppl.]
RC480.55.B453 1987   616.89'14   87–23865
ISBN 0–918863–01–5

C.P.S., Inc.
P.O. Box 83
Larchmont, N.Y. 10538

Printed in the United States of America

Cover Design: Robert Grossman

Library of Congress Catalog Number: 87–23865
International Standard Book Number: 0–918863–01–5

Introductory Note: This *Manual* is meant to be used in conjunction with the *Handbook of Intensive Brief and Emergency Psychotherapy (B.E.P.)*. The latter provides a theoretical framework; the Manual provides the actual words and phrases which might be useful for initiating and carrying on the psychotherapeutic process. The overall goal is to put the patient at ease and to get at the crucial details of what ails him and what brings him to us. The following suggestions are meant to help initiate the therapeutic process, the alliance, the contract, the transference situation, and to provide a guide for bringing the therapeutic process to successful completion.

* * *

A *Recording Blank for B.E.P.** is also available. It is also keyed to the headings in the Manual and the Handbook itself and permits use as a further simplified guide as well as a permanent record of the therapeutic data and process.

* * *

THE INITIAL SESSION

Chief Complaint

1. Would you tell me what brought you here?
2. When did you first think of seeking some help?
3. Why just then?
4. What had happened on that particular day or the day before?
5. Where exactly were you when you decided to come here?
6. What were you thinking at the moment you reached for the phone?

History of Chief Complaint

1. What would you say is your main problem?
2. When did it start?
3. What were you doing at the time? What was the setting you were in?
4. Did you ever have the same problem (depression, anxiety) before? When?
5. When was the first time you felt that way?
6. What was going on in your life then?
7. Was there any change in some aspect of your life (friends, work, family, etc.)?

Secondary Complaints

1. What else would you say troubles you?
2. When did that first begin to trouble you?
3. What were the circumstances?
4. How much does it interfere with your life?

Life History

1. Would you mind telling me your life history? Start right at the beginning.
2. Where were you born?
3. What was the family like?
4. Could you describe your father in three adjectives or traits?
5. Could you describe your mother in three adjectives or traits?
6. Did you have siblings? What were the age differences? Miscarriages? Dead siblings?
7. How did you get along with your siblings?
8. Where did you sleep? Where did everybody else sleep?
9. What was the general family atmosphere?
10. Who else played an important role in your life?
11. How did you get along in school?
12. Was school difficult for you?

13. Did you have any specific learning problems?
14. How did you do socially? In the gym?
15. Did you have friends? Were you a shy child? An overactive one?
16. How far did you go in school? Where?
17. What kind of medical illnesses do you have? Were you ever hospitalized?
18. What kind of medical illness did you have in infancy? Early childhood?
19. Have you had any operations? What kind?
20. Did you suffer from high fevers in childhood? Convulsions? What has your mother told you about your infancy and childhood?
21. Are you taking any drugs prescribed by a doctor at this time?
22. When did you have your last visit?
23. What street drugs are you taking? LSD? Speed? Crack? Coke? Pot? Alcohol? Mescaline?
24. What kinds of experiences did you have with these drugs? How did they make you feel?

Note: After taking this much history, you have to try and make some of your first tentative inferences as to what ails the patient and what played a role in the development of the chief complaint? Somatic? Developmental? Psychodynamic? What are the common denominators among the chief complaint and the history of the chief complaint and the secondary complaints and the life history and, for that matter, the family history.

Family History

1. Where did your parents come from? What was their background? How did they get along?
2. What kind of work did they do?
3. Did they have any particular emotional problems?
4. What kind?
5. Do any of your siblings have any particular emotional problems?
6. What are your siblings doing? Are they married?
7. Did they have any school problems?
8. Were any of them left-handed?
9. Did anyone in your family have temper outbursts?
10. Does anyone else in the family (aunts, uncles, cousins, parents, etc.) have any particular emotional problems? Do they get depressed? Are they sometimes overactive?
11. Has anyone in the family ever been hospitalized for a psychiatric problem?
12. What physical illnesses do you know of in the family?

Dynamic and Structural Formulation

Note: You want to have some tentative hypothesis of what makes this patient tick in the particular way he does, and why he or she is just that way. You may further, particularly with the more disturbed patient, attempt at this time to evaluate how well he is functioning. The scheme of 12 ego functions* may be useful at this point. You will want to briefly test the patient's ego functions with the help of the accompanying table (reality testing, judgement, impulse control, thought processes, etc.) and also to get an idea at this point of how capable the patient is of insight, whether there is some psychological mindedness or concrete thinking.

At this point, you will want to have some first tentative thoughts about a treatment plan—the *areas of intervention*, the *methods of intervention* you are going to choose, and what *sequence of areas and methods of intervention* you are planning to use.*

Transference

Note: As part of this hard work of the initial session, you will also now want to get an idea of the *transference* feelings on the part of the patient. There are two main sources for getting an idea as to what transference problems the patient is most likely to bring. One source is the *Life History*. If you hear of a life history in which someone has been distrustful of others all along, chances are that the patient will be distrustful towards you. The other source for indications as to the nature of the transference relationship is *Dreams*.

1. What did you dream last night?

   Note: If the patient cannot recall a dream from the previous night, you might ask

2. What recent dream can you recall?

   Note: If that doesn't work, or in addition to it

3. Can you tell me of *any* dream you have had in the course of your life?
4. In particular, can you recall any dreams from your childhood?
5. Have you ever had any *repetitive* dreams?

Note: If the patient can relate any of these, you will get a good idea of what the main dynamics might be. With regard to particular transference problems: If the patient has dreamt repetitively of being pursued by some monster, the helpless feeling vis a vis it, chances are that the patient will have similar feelings towards you, and you will have to keep in mind dealing with those fearful expectations of being overwhelmed and feeling helpless.

Use of Projective Devices

Note: Some patients will have a hard time relating any data and report that they do not have dreams. In such a case, to get the patient started, you might ask

---

* In: Handbook of Intensive Brief and Emergency Psychotherapy 2nd and Revised Edition (Bellak) C.P.S., Inc., Box 83, Larchmont, NY 10538.

1. Well, could you just describe for me what your day was like yesterday and today so far?
2. Well, how did you feel when this or that happened?

Note: You may be able to use some of the incidents described for interpretation. Another method is to use some kind of projective device to get at underlying material. One means available to everybody is a relatively blank piece of wall. One can ask the patient:

3. Could you, in your mind, draw a picture on that wall?
4. Well, now that you have a picture there, could you tell me a story about it?

Note: Let's assume that the patient has drawn a beach or an island, with palm trees, waves coming into shore, and a sailboat. One might point out:

5. All this is wonderful, but there are no people.

Note: In this way, one can point out that apparently the patient has little relationship to people. Having made that point, we can now ask him to try and introduce some people into the picture, and see whom he introduces, and what he has to tell about them, how they get along, how they feel about each other, etc.

If one has the TAT or CAT pictures available, it is useful to utilize whatever picture seems most likely to illuminate the patient's problems. If there are family problems, Picture #2 of the TAT, of a farm scene, might usefully illuminate the nature of the conflicts. There are two or three pictures (3BM, 10, 13M) which lend themselves to themes of aggression, and one might use them to point out common denominators in the stories, as the patient relates them.

One might use a concrete event, an historical event, from the patient's life, as well as a dream or projective production, as a series of common denominators to be interpreted. In the CAT, the picture suggesting animals or people sleeping together in one room or a cave may bring out oedipal problems, etc.

With regard to the TAT pictures, the instructions would be:

6. Could you tell me a story about what is going on, what lead up to it, and what the outcome will be? You can just make it a simple story.

Therapeutic Alliance

Note: You will want to establish a therapeutic alliance. At this point you might say to the patient:

1. Look, you obviously came here because you know that something ails you. That means that there is one part of you which has problems and another part that is intelligent and knows that something is wrong and that something needs to be done about it. I need the intelligent, competent, healthy part of you to sit together with me, and both of us will try to understand the childlike part of you that is causing the problems.

4

Note: At this point, you might use the following technique:

2. Look, you have just told me a great deal. If we would mentally reverse chairs now, and you would be the psychiatrist who has just listened to all this, what kind of notions might you have as to what ails this person?

Note: This is an attempt to introduce some psychological-mindedness, some awareness, and to initiate a therapeutic alliance in starting the process of therapy.

Therapeutic Contract

Note: The patient is entitled to have a therapeutic contract. He is entitled to have some idea of what is in store for him. Spell it out now:

1. We are going to meet once a week, all other things being equal, for about an hour a week, and it has been my experience that meeting for five times is useful and then, after we are all done, and hopefully, you'll be feeling much better, I will still want to hear from you or see you a month later for a sixth session. If, by chance, you should not feel markedly better or even all right, it will be my job to help see that you get more treatment. If I can't provide it, it will be my job to introduce you to somebody who can carry on and we will sit together, all three of us, and I'll fill in the other therapist on what we have learned and you might want to add things yourself and then you two will take over from there. That way you don't have to start from scratch with an unknown person.

Review and Planning

Note: Since the patient feels overwhelmed by whatever ails him, it's important to give him an idea that we "can understand" what his problems are about, and have some notions as to what can be done about them, other than just plain talking. I would review the information briefly, and point out one or two common denominators that relate to the patient's problems and explain to him that we will want to go into these problems in more detail. For example

1. When you were 5, you felt deserted by your parents, when they went out in the evening. At 12, you suffered from fears of being alone at the time that your parents decided to divorce. You had similar fears when you went away to college. What do all these situations have in common? [the problem (fear) of being alone]. Being "left" seems to be a lifelong problem of yours and now you carry over that fear to our treatment, and are very scared of being left by me. We will want to be aware that some of these fears might make you temporarily worse, until we can understand them.

SECOND SESSION

Note: In this second session, we explore further, get better closure, and reexamine the basis for choosing areas and methods of intervention.

1. How are you feeling today?
2. How have you been feeling since you were last here?
3. What has happened in your life since then?
4. What did you dream the night after you had been here?
5. What did you dream last night?
6. What thoughts did you have as you left the last session?
7. What has occurred to you that you should also mention?
8. Did anything of what we discussed stay in your mind?
9. Did our discussion make sense to you at all?
10. In essence, what we arrived at was . . .   . I wonder if you have any other thoughts about that?
11. Did you think of any other things that trouble you?
12. A few things weren't quite clear to me—in your complaints, in your history, at the end of the last session, etc. (Review again briefly the main things learned in that session and relate it to the patient's main problems.)

THIRD SESSION

1. How are you feeling today?
2. How have you been feeling since I last saw you?

   Note: If the patient has difficulties in relating significant data, keep in mind the variables mentioned under *The Therapeutic Process* and *Methods of Intervention.*
   Also keep in mind the specific variables mentioned for certain conditions such as depression, acting out, etc., and intervene as specifically indicated for these conditions.
   In the third session, about the middle of it, it is time to start referring to the *impending separation* that will occur in the fifth session. At that time, one can expect a resurgence of some symptoms that might have already decreased because of the feared separation. It is valuable here to say:

3. You know, this is our third session. We have another two and then we will have a sixth session about a month later, and I will want to hear about how you are doing. Of course, you can talk to me sooner if you are not feeling all right. But I will want to hear from you a month after our last session even if you are feeling perfectly all right. If you are not feeling well, it will be my job to see that you get

6

further treatment, if not by me, then by somebody else whom we both put in the picture (this should be part of the contract made at the end of the first hour).

Note: One might also say to the patient

4. You know, I wouldn't be surprised if you might possibly feel worse again in some ways by next week, simply because you may feel that I am deserting you and in some ways you feel scared about having to go it alone. But I am telling you this in the hope of avoiding that sort of reaction.

FOURTH SESSION

Note: We repeat many of the same things we have said in all other sessions:

1. How do you feel?
2. How have you been feeling since last time?
3. What has happened in your life?
4. What did you think of the last session?
5. What did you dream after the last session?
6. What did you dream last night?
7. What other dreams have you had since I've last seen you?

Note: We should remind the patient again that the next session will be our last one except for the follow-up session, and we work through whatever comes up in connection with separation anxiety, or any of the other problems that played a crucial role in the patient's complaints.

FIFTH SESSION

1. How are you feeling today?
2. How have you been feeling since I last saw you?
3. Well, what would you say you have learned?
4. Could you give me a review of the things that we have found out?

Note: I would supplement important points which the patient has left out and then say:

5. After all the many questions I have asked you, what questions would you like to ask me?
6. I told you that if you should need further treatment I will be unable to continue to see you, but I will introduce you to somebody competent who will continue treatment with you. I will introduce you to one of my colleagues (in the clinic, agency, etc.) and, with your permission, we three will sit together and I'll review what we have learned and then you two can take off from there.

Note: This is said, in part, because it's usually true, and also to indicate to the patient that he will not be abandoned, and also to avoid continued symptoms due to transference dependence.

Unlike other sessions, I would engage in some relatively informal chatting about current events, or whatever might be of interest. The idea here is to end treatment on a positive note. That involves the giving up of some of the therapeutic neutrality and relating as human being to human being.

SIXTH SESSION: FOLLOW-UP

The sixth session is the follow-up session, taking place approximately one month after the fifth session.

We ask extensively how the patient has been feeling generally, and especially with regard to his specific symptoms:

1. How would you say you have been feeling generally?
2. Are you still at all depressed (anxious, etc.)

   If the patient reports that things are well with him, we leave him with a positive transference, if at all possible, saying

3. "I would always like to hear from you if there is any problem or you can send me a postcard even a year from now. I will be very interested to hear how you are doing."

Note: If the patient should not be feeling well, or have significant symptoms remaining, or if the patient calls between the 5th and the 6th session, we have to offer him more help, as mentioned above.

Altogether, speaking of 6-session therapy is just a matter of convenience and practicality. Some patients may do well with just 4 sessions and some may need 10. If you cannot continue to see the patient, you have to provide somebody who will take over, introducing the patient to that individual (see Therapeutic Contract).

THE THERAPEUTIC PROCESS

Note: In Brief Therapy, we do not wait until the patient has something to say or sit back and just hum occasionally. We start out by saying:

1. Well, tell me what all has happened in your life. What has been upsetting?

   Note: If the patient doesn't have much to say, I might ask:

2. Well, what was the first thing you thought when you woke up this morning?
3. How did you feel then?
4. What were the thoughts you were preoccupied with as you were sitting out in the waiting room?
5. What did you think about when you were riding on the bus this morning?
6. While you were shaving?
7. While you were putting on your make-up?
8. When you went to sleep?

   If none of the above helps, I would say:

9. Well, just give me an idea of what you did yesterday.

   Note: As I listen to the patient's report of his day I would, at some point, say

10. Well, what were you thinking or feeling when you were doing . . . ?

    Note: If we have a quite disturbed patient who, for instance, has dreams in pure primary process of a very frightening nature, and is inclined to produce more such material with increasing upset, I would say:

11. Well, I guess these are pretty upsetting things. But they'll disappear. Tell me how you spent your day and what you are planning for the rest of the week.

    Note: In other words, I am trying to dilute the pressure by talking about concrete things and interpreting only selected problems. The style and form of delivery is important here. If the patient had a dream or an hallucination of being chased by a huge animal, you might just say:

12. Well, that must have been pretty scary. It must be something from your childhood that is bothering you. But of course everybody has nightmares sometimes.

Explaining the Therapeutic Process

Note: In part, the patient does not know just what is expected of him or her and *we do have to define the task for the patient* as well as explain the therapeutic process. It is necessary to do this at intervals, to maintain as good a working alliance as possible. I would say something like the following:

13. Look, something troubles you, and what we need to understand is how you got this way. It doesn't come about by accident and there must have been things that made you feel this way (scared, depressed, anxious, etc.). By trying to understand your life history, we get an idea of what all might be causing the things that trouble you now. Since there are no accidents in mental life anymore than there are in the physical world: there must be a reason why this book falls down, namely because of gravity. So too there must be a reason why you are thinking certain thoughts or doing certain things. If we can understand the reasons why and also understand that originally you might have not been able to understand what scared you . . . and you are still seeing things in a way similar to the way you saw them through your childhood eyes, then we can sort of try and correct your vision. Once we can do that, these things will stop being as scary or as upsetting as they are to you now.

Note: One has to explain to the patient that all contemporary experiences are seen, in part, in terms of contemporary problems and also, in part, are structured by past experiences. You can tell the story of the experiment by Chen, Levin, and Murphy.

14. In a famous experiment ten students were starved for 24 hours as volunteers, while ten other students were allowed to eat normally. Following this, they were shown the same exact pictures in a tachistoscope, something like a camera, and the pictures were exposed only for one hundredth of a second or so. It turned out that the students who were starved saw food much more often in the pictures than the ones who were not hungry. *That goes to show that one's emotions have a good deal to do with what one sees and how one interprets what one sees.*

Note: To explain the concept of *Projection:*

15. One man's car broke down as his tire deflated and he needed a jack. He didn't have one but he knew there was a gas station about two miles away from where he was and he decided to walk there and get the jack. As he was walking along, he began to get tired and hot and bothered and angry and said to himself: "That son-of-a-bitch at the gas station! I betcha he'll charge me two bucks just to lend me the jack."

As he walked further, his feet began to hurt him and he said to himself: "That son-of-a-bitch at the gas station! He knows he got me! There's nobody else around and I need that jack . . . he'll either want a deposit or he might even charge me 10 bucks! That God-damn-son-of-a-bitch!" He kept on muttering about this God-damn-son-of-a-bitch and what he was going to charge him, how unpleasant he would be, and then he finally reached the gas station. The attendant there said, "Yes, sir, what can I do for you?" The man replied, "You can take your God-damned jack and shove it!"

Note: To explain the concept of *Ambivalence:*

16. That's for instance when a guy's mother-in-law drives off the road in his new Cadillac . . . he has mixed feelings.

   Note: To explain *Self-Reporting and Insight:*

17. Once a young delinquent was being prepared by a social worker for a consultation with me. When she asked him if he knew what a psychiatrist was, he replied, "Sure, he's the guy what makes you squeal on yourself." Well, that's just what we need here. I need you to squeal on yourself. You observe yourself and then tell me what all goes on in you.

   Note: If the patient has great problems with awareness of the subjective nature of his disturbances, you might use one or two TAT plates and have him tell stories to the pictures, and then show him how other people might have told other stories and that there are, in fact, some common denominators in his stories. That way, you might begin the process of insight and perception of individual differences.

Structuring Effect of Past Experience

Note: With regard to the projection story, you can explain to the patient that sometimes we run around with a mental set and feelings that can distort what we perceive with regard to a wife, a boss, whatever. In the jack story, the man's own expectations colored his perceptions so that he didn't even gather that the station attendant was being quite courteous and hadn't made any demand whatsoever. He just expected it.

In this sense, therapy is a form of correcting our vision, doing away with the distortions that we have acquired when we were much younger.

18. You know, from birth on, and maybe even before that, we perceive things: mother feeding, mother scolding, father being scary, a younger sibling being a pest, etc.

   All our experiences are like pieces in a kaleidoscope, or like photographic transparencies. They overlay each other and when we look at a contemporary person, we see them distorted by these past experiences and perceptions. That is why some people are especially scared of a boss—if father was scary—or why some men see a woman as bossy if their mother was, etc.

   In part, our job is to understand what past experiences have affected you and formed your impressions of people—and yourself—and then with the help of your adult intelligence we can try and restructure them. Psychotherapy is nothing more than a form of unlearning, learning, and relearning.

METHODS OF INTERVENTION

Interpretation

1. Look, you told me that you get your kicks out of scaring girls by exposing yourself. You also like to upset them with obscene phone calls and then you had this dream of knocking over a whole set of bowling pins. What do you think these three instances might have in common?

   Note: Help the patient to see the common denominator, namely: The wish to be strong, scary, powerful.

Catharsis

1. Well, tell me how you actually felt when such and such happened. You're telling it to me as if you were giving me a weather report. One would not be able to guess that you actually felt terribly angry or terribly hurt or terribly unhappy. I can't hear it in your voice. It doesn't show in your face. How was it really? How did you really feel? Tell me in detail.
2. And what did you do, in detail, when you felt that way?

Mediate Catharsis

1. If this had happened to me, I certainly would have felt extremely angry and would have wanted to call him a "son-of-a-bitch." Or I would have been very unhappy and complained about the unfairness. But you have such a strict conscience, you couldn't say what you really felt or thought.
2. You might have thought, "He should drop dead!" But with your strict conscience, you don't even permit yourself to have such thoughts, while in fact most other people would have just those thoughts.

Auxiliary Reality Testing

1. You know, when one person tells you that you're drunk, you can disregard it. When two people tell you, you might still not pay attention. But when three tell you the same thing, you had better start taking it easy.

Drive Repression

1. Well, just because all the other kids use crack, are promiscuous, cheat, etc. is no reason why you should have to do it or be that way. You have your rules and they have theirs and there is no reason why you should feel obliged to behave the way they do.

2. Everyone has to live within the means of his/her conscience, just as one has to live within one's financial means and if one exceeds those, one feels bad and that is what happened to you.
3. So you had some very angry thoughts, but that's only human. I don't think those thoughts are terribly important.

Sensitization to Signals

1. When you notice that you are breathing faster, or talking faster, laughing too much . . . that could be a signal to you that you are about to fly off the handle, that you are tense, that you might do something impulsive.
2. If you notice that you don't want to get out of bed in the morning, that you don't feel like shopping in the supermarket, that you don't want to cook for your family, you should remind yourself that that often is an early symptom of your being depressed, and you had better come in or start your medication.
3. If you feel like fighting with your husband and are generally cross, look at the calendar and see if you are not premenstrual. Then try to discount the things that upset you and decrease your water intake and leave whatever you need to discuss until after your period starts.

Education

1. That pain you get in your chest when you get tense is not the type of pain one gets from a coronary or from angina. That doesn't mean that it is imaginary. What happens is that the small muscles between the ribs tighten up and that can cause quite a bit of pain and discomfort, without being anything serious.

Intellectualization

1. Well, it may not be so easy to actually change your behavior, but at least you ought to understand why you are scared sometimes to drive to work, or to walk across the street. It's a condition which many people suffer from. It's called agoraphobia. There are different opinions about what may cause it in one person or another, but chances are that it's a fear to leave home. I wonder if you weren't afraid as a kid to go to school sometimes, and if you didn't sometimes think that your mother might die while you were away or that something terrible might happen to you on the way.
2. You know, what ails you now is really very similar to what troubled you as a kid, and if you'll just keep in mind that it's an irrational condition that goes back to childhood, it won't cure the problem but it will make it a little bit more bearable, until we can do something more basic about it.

Supportive Statements

1. Well, this symptom makes you feel helpless and like a fool. The fact is that you have led a pretty successful life, have discharged all kinds of responsibilities, and

are healthy enough to have realized that this is peculiar and have come here for help. I have certainly seen worse, which doesn't mean that I am fluffling off what ails you, but you should keep in mind that you are not the only one suffering from such a problem, and that one can usually treat it successfully.

Conjoint Sessions and Family Network Therapy

1. Well, I think you two have a communication problem and we need to get a dialogue going. If both of you could come here, I could help get you two started on discussing what is really wrong between you two, and I might be able to point out a few things, and we can all learn together.
2. What ails you is not your problem alone. When you feel unhappy the rest of the family teases you or complains about your depression, which in turn makes you angry. Of course, when you don't feel like doing anything, it makes all the others angry, so it's really important that we get the whole family here and get everybody's feelings aired and understood.

Psychoactive Drugs

1. I would like you to take this medication. It's not going to perform any miracles. In the first place, it may take a week or ten days for the medication to have any effect (tricyclics). Also, it doesn't do away with the reasons for your depression, which we are hoping our talking, our psychotherapy, will do. If it doesn't help at all, I hope it will help for you to tell me what all ails you and why. And once we understand things, you can stop taking this medication.
2. It may possibly cause acute side effects. The most frequent (talking about tricyclics) are dry throat, dry mouth, sometimes a little bit of blurred vision), but in the small amounts that you are getting, it may not happen at all. If your vision is affected, don't drive. If you have any other side effect, stop taking the drug and call me or your internist.

   It is very unlikely that you will have other side effects from it, though any drug that is powerful enough to help is also powerful enough to possibly cause some trouble.
3. This drug will help you feel less anxious when you are walking around or taking an elevator or flying. It doesn't do away with those anxieties, but it enables you to do the things that frighten you and we get a chance to try and understand what is troubling you. And the more you are in the situation that scares you, the more grist it is for our mill, unpleasant as it is, in trying to understand what goes on in you. So the drugs are more than just a temporary band-aid. They actually help us deal with the basics of your condition.

THE USE OF DREAMS IN BRIEF THERAPY

Note: In Brief Therapy, we utilize primarily, if not exclusively, the manifest dream for gaining and furthering insight. Only occasionally will the unsophisticated patient, not accustomed to free associating, supply data comparable to free associations.

You can say to the patient:

1. What did you dream last night?

Note: If the patient replies, "Nothing," we say:

2. Well, it doesn't have to be a whole drama. Can you recall anything—a face, a place, a feeling?

Note: This way, many a patient who at first says that he or she had no dreams may eventually relate a long one. If that doesn't work, we say:

3. What kind of recent dream do you remember?
4. What dream did you have earlier in the week?
5. What dream did you have last week?

Note: After this, whether the question was answered positively or not, you can ask:

6. What kind of dream can you remember from your childhood?
7. Did you have any recurrent dreams?
8. Did you have any recurrent nightmares?

Note: Especially recurrent dreams or early childhood ones are likely to give a very good picture of the main anxieties, the main dynamics.

It is very easy to utilize the manifest dream. If a patient dreams that there was a very heavy weight on him, I might, for instance, just translate that as:

9. Gee, you must have really felt weighted down by the demands of your parents (if he was relating the dream in connection with a discussion of parental expectations).

Note: A man related a dream about being in bed with his girlfriend, lying spoon-fashion, while another man with whom he worked was having intercourse with her from the front. The patient reported that he felt annoyed in the dream. This dream lends itself to pointing out:

10. Looks like you feel quite competitive with that fellow and it looks like you feel you're getting screwed, losing out. It is quite curious that you should feel only annoyed.

Note: This might then lead into a discussion of his need to deny, since one could have expected that he would be much more upset, much angrier about this. What one does here is to just utilize one aspect of the dream and leave out whatever deeper sexual significance there might be, such as the latent homosexuality, etc. If a patient reports dreams of being pursued by a large animal, one might ask:

11.   I wonder who that might be? Who comes to your mind?

Note: And if the gorilla looks a little bit like mother, one could say:

12   Well, you must have been terribly scared of her when you were a kid to dream of her in that form.

Note: The more dreams, the more common denominators one can find, the better the chances for meaningful interpretations and insight, and working through on the part of the patient.

DEPRESSION

General Questions

1. Tell me what brings you here.
2. When did it start?
3. Do you remember which exact month it was, not just last summer or last spring? Which day? Where were you when you started to feel depressed?
4. When did you first notice it?
5. What was going on in your life?
6. Have you ever felt that way before?
7. When was the first time?
8. What was going on in your life then?
9. What about the other times?
10. Have you ever felt very high also?
11. Were there times when you didn't need very much sleep?
12. Did people tell you that you were talking loud?
13. Did you feel generally restless?
14. When you say depressed, what do you mean?
15. Is it hard for you to get up in the morning?
16. Is your appetite poor?
17. Are you constipated?
18. Do you sleep more in the daytime than at night?
19. Is it hard for you to do things?
20. Do you feel like you don't have very much energy?
21. Do you feel slowed up?
22. Do you feel sometimes that life is not worth living?
23. Have you thought about suicide? How?
24. What did you think about how you would do it?
25. How close have you come to it?
26. What were your thoughts about being dead?
27. How would your family and your friends react?

Problems of Self-Esteem Regulation

1. What is it that made you feel so bad about yourself?
2. Why did that have such a devastating effect on you and would likely have had little effect on someone else?
3. I wonder what in your life history made you have such a low self-esteem and made you think so little of yourself? What made you feel so small and helpless?

4. It sounds like you still feel that way about yourself, or at least one part of you feels that way about yourself, as if you were still that small child that was helpless, afraid of being criticized?

5. Now that your mother and your father can't criticize you anymore, you are just doing it to yourself. It is as if you had built in their view of you, as if you had been conditioned, programmed like a computer, to be self-critical.

6. Just what are your expectations of yourself that you feel you are falling so woefully short?

7. Why do you feel you have to be so big, so successful, invulnerable?

8. What makes you feel so small that you have to make yourself feel so big?

Severe Superego

1. How did you get to be as critical of yourself as you are?

2. Who in your life behaved that way towards you?

3. Do you think you are critical towards yourself the way your mother used to be toward you?

4. Do you feel guilty about practically everything?

5. It sounds to me like you have a very, very severe conscience that pinches you all the time. Sometimes you even feel guilty for things that aren't even your responsibility.

6. When you have reason to be angry, you often don't let yourself do anything about it. You just keep on smiling, while you really have murder in your heart. The reason you get depressed is because you are a very conscientious and decent person who doesn't even permit himself to think vicious thoughts, leave alone to do vicious things. It's as though you hit out at an opponent and then have it reflected against yourself.

7. And now you ascribe all those critical feelings to me and think that I am sitting here in judgement of you. Now you think that I am a bad person, because really you go around as if you were looking through a set of glasses and seeing everybody in terms of those glasses as being critical of you.

Intra-Aggression

1. I wonder whom you are really angry at?

2. It seems that you are angry at yourself, but I think you are doing that because it is easier than permitting yourself to be angry at others.

3. It is as if a little bit of your critical grandmother would be sitting right inside your head and go on criticizing you, and you, of course, don't dare be critical of her, because that would make you feel that you're a bad grandchild.

4. That's why you have to be so extra-good, to make sure that everybody is all right, because that one part in you criticizes you all the time and doesn't permit you any rest.

5. You know, sometimes when one would really like to punch somebody, or tear out their hair, one grabs one's own hair or punches oneself instead. You might say

that in such a case, the anger that is meant for the other person is turned against oneself. If one does a good deal of this, and is critical of oneself, it can make one feel quite depressed. One just simply feels that one is no good.

Is *that* the sort of thing that happens to you sometimes?

6. Even suicidal ideas can be of this nature. Unreasonable as it sounds, some people sometimes have ideas of killing themselves because they hope that that will make all their survivors, all the people they are angry at, feel very guilty and unhappy and full of regret. They are sort of willing to cut off their noses to spite their faces.

Loss

1. You know, when your parents divorced, you lost a parent. And when the grandmother you loved died, you were also experiencing a loss. And now that you have retired (lost your job, etc.) it is once more a loss, a function you don't have any more, a job you don't have any more, and you react to it with unhappiness, with a depression, the same way that you reacted to earlier losses. Aside from being sad, which is understandable, losing somebody one loves or something one loves also makes one angry too. And if you lose your job, it also makes you feel less important, hurts your self-esteem. It is as if part of yourself were lost, and you feel weaker, smaller. You feel literally bereft, diminished. And, of course, the more that one needs people, the more one loves somebody, the more painful the loss is.

2. Because you have had these earlier losses, you are all the more eager to hold on to what you have and react all the more to another loss or the threat of a loss.

3. You know, you were quite disappointed that your parents showed so much interest in your younger sister; because she was a preemie, they had to pay particular attention to her, but all you could understand when you were three years old was that suddenly they were paying less attention to you and too much attention to her.

4. You must have felt deceived, thinking that they loved you and then, bingo, they bring in a competitor.

5. And then later on, when you had to switch schools, you felt again deserted, disappointed. You had achieved a certain status in the first school and had friends, and then you lost all that. And then you developed all these ambitions—of wanting to be rich and famous. I guess all this was supposed to make up for your previous disappointments.

6. And then you loaded the dice against yourself and practically *arranged* to be disappointed because you had such unreasonably high expectations. And now that such and such happened, you feel once more disappointed, in the same way, let down.

7. And all you can see are the negative things in your life—you practically have what we call *"tunnel vision,"* as if you would look down the world through a narrow tube and only see this last disappointment, instead of the rest of the world.

8. If you'll take that tube away and look around yourself, you'll also see that you did accomplish quite a bit—that you have lots of reason to feel satisfied and happy, but that you simply have the wrong perspective because of your previous experiences of disappointment. It is as if you would have become sensitized or *allergic* to disappointment and then even a little bit of it sets you back and makes you depressed.

9. As a matter of fact, you are approaching *this treatment* already expecting to be disappointed. You expect me not to do much for you, you expect to fail at it, you come here with a very negative outlook. Instead of saying that you're going to try your best to understand what ails you, you are only too likely to feel hopeless about this also and to insist that I am just one more person who is going to disappoint you.

10. And, of course, every time that you were disappointed, you were enraged. You felt let down, so I won't be too surprised if some of that anger also shows against me. For instance, you came to your session late today. And I wonder if that was your way of paying me back in advance, disappointing me by not showing up, or by showing up late. Your dream shows disappointment. Several of the stories that you told me in relation to the picture I showed you in essence deal with the theme of disappointment. Other people, in contrast, see totally different things in the pictures.

11. You will have to unlearn looking at the world as a source of disappointment, as you have from childhood to now, and learn to enjoy the good things in your life.

Deception

1. I wonder if you didn't feel deceived when they brought your little brother home from the hospital. At first, he seemed like a nice toy for you, and then you found out that that little baby demanded a great deal of attention from your parents, and cried a good deal, and that made you feel you were being left out in the cold. It made you expect that the whole world might deceive you and you have been cautious ever since, practically looking around and behind you to see if anybody else might be deceiving you.

2. That experience made you quite suspicious. You feel you can't trust anybody. It also makes you quite jealous, and you expect to be deceived by your spouse also. And whenever you feel deceived, you then feel depressed. Once more you have proven to yourself that the world is no good and has it in for you, that one can't trust anybody.

Orality and Stimulus Hunger

1. I guess you literally felt you didn't get "enough" from your mother. Of course, now you understand that she had to go to work to help support the family and things were tough economically, but all you understood *at the time* was that she wasn't there, that she turned you over to the nursery (the neighbor, grandmother,

20

aunt, whomever). It has made you want to have life make up for that early deprivation, and it is as if you often want just to be taken care of, to be given a big breast, not to have to actively go after things yourself, but rather to be taken care of.

2. I think that shows here too, in your expectations about your therapy. In your dream, you are the little baby who is being carried around and given the bottle and here, in essence, you want me to hand you solutions rather than having to work to get them. Somehow, you expect a magic cure that will make you satisfied forever, when the fact is that it's part of life to sometimes have satisfaction and not at other times. In addition, when you feel dissatisfied, you make up for what you felt you lost when your sibling was born and you became depressed by stuffing yourself with sweets.

3. When you go to the refrigerator, it is really as if you were saying, "I wasn't fed enough, nobody feeds me enough, I have to take loving care of myself, and that's when you can't stop stuffing yourself. That's why you like to take big gulps and to have your cheeks full, so that you really feel the fullness, rather than the emptiness. And whenever you feel empty, psychologically, for one reason or another, you try and fill up the void by stuffing yourself, or by drinking, or by taking drugs. It is as if you would want to devour a great deal when you don't feel like simply lying down and being taken care of.

    Note: I remember a patient who didn't get enough to eat when he was small and would have daydreams of eating his way through a barn full of ice cream. Another had the fantasy that he would be cooped up in a hotel room and could buzz room service for whatever he might want, including friends and sex partners. Sort of "feeding by demand" or "instant gratification."

4. And sometimes you simply need a lot of people around you, or even loud music or a lot of activity, because that also makes you feel filled up, helps you deal with that feeling of emptiness inside you. Or you get frantic and want to do a great deal, also an attempt to fill yourself up.

Narcissism

1. Because you feel you have been disappointed, deceived, not given enough, you feel you have to take particularly good care of yourself. In a way, that often means that you are not really interested in other people or other things, and that is an outstanding part of your feeling depressed, a lack of interest. Unfortunately, that, in turn, then becomes disturbing to you. Because you feel bored, you feel you don't want to get up, you feel uninterested in anything else. But that's really the result of your being, to start with, exclusively interested in yourself.

2. You feel good only if people admire you, praise you, because originally, you felt bad about yourself, felt disappointed, felt deceived, inadequate, etc. In a way, you behave a little bit the way the so-called "cold-blooded animals" feel, in comparison to the "warm-blooded" ones. The so-called cold-blooded ones, when they are in a freezing environment, their blood temperature or body temperature is quite low,

21

and when the snake lies in the sun, then the body temperature can get quite high. Now, with people, we have a thermostat built into the mid-brain, and our temperature, when we are healthy, stays more or less at 98.6, maybe going down a couple of points when we are out in the freezing winter, and going up a few points if we are lying on a hot beach. But, by and large, it is regulated from the inside, regardless of what the outside temperature is like.

3. Now, you are emotionally a bit like the cold-blooded animal. When people love you, you can feel very good—your emotional temperature goes up. When there is nobody there to say that you are wonderful, or you have an adverse experience, the temperature goes down like the snake's does—for a whole day. If we can get you to be less dependent on the outside emotional temperature, and think more kindly of yourself, then you won't be as dependent on daily events. You won't get depressed if something adverse happens, because you'll look more kindly on yourself and have a better opinion of yourself, so as not to be as readily affected by others.

4. *Sensitization:* It's important that you understand how such insults to your feeling of importance affect you so that you at least can anticipate when you are likely to react with a feeling of depression or unhappiness, that is once more an injury to your self-esteem. And, with a little bit of luck, you might be able to *predict* how you might react appropriately, and avoid the feeling of depression.

5. Or maybe if we can work through sufficiently how these feelings of disappointment and of lowered self-esteem, of a feeling of loss, of a feeling of not being important, affect you, then perhaps this won't happen to you anymore. If all goes well, you'll have a good thermostat built in that makes sure that your emotional temperature stays more even than it has been so far, because you have a better sense of yourself.

Denial

1. You know, what you do is to try simply not to see whatever might be painful or disappointing. I think you can become alert to that process in yourself because you usually start with fantasies of being a great man or woman, "macho," admired like a movie star. I think you might learn that as a giveaway, that you have these thoughts to start with as an attempt to deny that right then and there you feel like a "schlemiel," unattractive, unwanted, or unsuccessful or gypped.

2. The fact is that *you don't have to make yourself so big; you are not really that small.* You behave like a guy who stands in front of the mirror and flexes his muscles, to make himself feel better about himself. But you aren't that puny. You are just particularly sensitive to *feeling* small, feeling disappointed, feeling deceived, because of the experiences in your childhood.

3. *Then* you were helpless. There was nothing you could do to make things better for yourself. But *now* that you are an intelligent adult, you can react more adaptively than by simply blotting out what upsets you, either by withdrawing or by feeling unhappy and depressed, or by being overly active—full of pretense and grandiose notions.

Object Relations

1. I guess with your disappointment in your mother you are trying to make up for it all along by having somebody hold your hand, lead you, support you. That plays a role here too. You are already worried about the end of your treatment and you'd really rather that I go along with you and have answers for you and help you solve your problems.

2. It's a little bit like a kid going to school for the first time and being scared to leave home and leave mother behind. Every relationship for you is like having to cut that umbilical cord again, and you're scared that you might not be able to make it on your own. It's as if you never quite left mother, and are trying to have substitute mothers. Once upon a time, that was understandable, and even served a sort of pseudo-function, since as a kid, you could, to a considerable extent, hold on to your mother.

3. Now in *adulthood* you don't need to hold on to mother, and that attitude does you a great deal of harm. It keeps you from being independent, from going places, from doing things as actively and as successfully as you might, based on your intelligence and general ability. But you still continue to feel like a dependent child and a helpless child, and are easily threatened, easily feel disappointed, deceived.

4. When you drew that figure of a man (patient was asked to draw a person), his hands were stretched out, as if you were always looking for somebody to hold on to. You are a perfectly competent, grown-up person, who can do it on his/her own, and that's part of the job we have—to have you learn that you can do it on your own.

ACTING OUT

Bargain for a Delay

1. Look, you'll do what you want to do (leave the job, jump out of the window, break up the marriage, etc.). It's *your life* and *your right* to do what you want to, and there is neither anything I want to do nor can do about it. But that also holds true for tomorrow or next week or next year. You still are the one to decide, still the one to do what you want to do. But meanwhile, it couldn't hurt to talk it over and get to understand better why you want to do what you want to do.

Make the Act Ego-Alien

1. You know, if you have a look at your life history, there are certain common denominators in how you react in situations in which you feel desperate, angry, let down or whatever. And there is a common denominator because your early experiences of disappointment, loss, etc., programmed you as if you were a computer. You have learned to react in this particular way and now the computer runs you.
2. You have the feeling that *you* are doing it, when actually something in you *makes you do it*. It's not really your choice.
3. You know, my favorite definition of mental health is having a choice—to have a choice of behavior, of response. You can choose to respond one way or another. But in your case, it really seems as if you have to go through a certain sequence which feels as if you are doing it, but actually it is your unconscious making you do it.

Cathartic Interpretation of the Underlying Drive

1. I know that sometimes it feels good to just blow one's stack. Say the hell with the consequences—this is what I'm going to do! Sometimes one is even a little bit aware that it's not the best thing to do before one does it, or even while one does it. It just simply feels good to get it out of one's system. Unfortunately, soon after that, one can feel remorse, regret, guilt, and be unhappy about the consequences.
2. Sometimes, something one does impulsively simply makes one feel big, important, and very soon after that, one feels foolish. In your case, you want to do such and such because it will make you feel such and such. If we look at it realistically, I can tell you that if you would go through with it, you will later wish that you had not.

Signal Awareness

1. You know, we are all, to a considerable extent, influenced as the result of learning. We learn to respond to any number of cues, for instance in a social situation. We stop at red lights and are courteous to our superiors and get angry at other drivers and are impatient with the bus driver and all kinds of other things.

2. Now, you happen to get into trouble when such and such happens. As soon as a woman smiles at you, you feel that you are in love and want to settle down for good, without really giving the relationship a chance to be checked out and then you find yourself practically claustrophobic and rapidly want out.

3. In your case, it's important that you realize that you get these overwhelming romantic feelings and keep in mind that it is good to check yourself and tell yourself to take your time and not to overcommit yourself. You have to recognize the signs, like an adolescent in Spring, especially when you feel lonely and you are too likely to over-react emotionally. So I want you to be aware of this and when you start having daydreams of a wonderful honeymoon trip, it's time to check yourself and to ask yourself if this is reasonable to act upon now. And if our treatment goes well, you will learn to be able to predict when you are likely to react this way, and after a while, this over-reaction will disappear and you'll be able to suspend judgement until you can act more reasonably.

Predict When the Patient Will Act Out

1. You know, we can count on the fact that whenever such and such happens in your life, you will react with what is practically a stereotyped response. For instance, you are going to take an examination now, and your tendency will be to get through with it as fast as possible and preferably be the first to leave the classroom. That's only because you can't stand the tension of going about it as carefully and slowly as possible and using every last minute to your advantage. Now, I predict that you'll feel that way again, wanting to get done and out, but I hope to be wrong. If you keep this in mind and recognize the signals then I hope I will have predicted wrongly.

Strengthen the Superego

1. You know, you say that you want to kill yourself by turning on the gas. But you haven't given any thought to how this might affect your little infant, how your parents will feel, how devastated your spouse will be. And what's more, somebody might strike a match and by accident blow up a good part of the building. And all this you are willing to risk because you feel bad. It really shows a serious lack of judgement and lack of conscience.

2. Everything that one does is likely to affect other people also, and from a civilized person, one can expect a certain amount of good judgement and responsibility playing a role in decisions which one thinks of as being primarily one's own.

Remove the Patient From a Provocative Setting

1. Look, the situation you are in is like sitting on a hot stove and trying to be well adjusted. That's pretty impossible. So the first thing for you to do is to move out of the place where all this tension arises, (to give up your gun, to avoid drinking, etc.) so that you should not find a provocation to easily act on your impulses. Because if you do act on impulse, it will cause all kinds of trouble, no doubt.

Enlist the Help of Others

1. Every once in a while, it's very difficult for any of us to control ourselves. That's what makes diet books so successful. Somebody else tells us just what we can eat and what we can't eat. That's why some people like to join the army, because it's quite clear what you are supposed to do and what you cannot do. It gives you structure. That's why free-lance artists have a particularly hard time sometimes, because they don't have to punch a clock and they can tell themselves, "If I start an hour later, it will be O.K. also," and then they may not get up at all.

2. Now, I think that you are in that sort of a situation. It's very difficult for you to control yourself on your own. Therefore, you need somebody who gets you out of bed and goes to school with you (who sees to it that you don't have liquor around, who is part of a regular schedule that you have to meet). You simply need somebody else, some circumstances, which will help to support your making a commitment.

Drugs

1. Look, what ails you is to a large extent an emotional problem, but you can't divide body and mind. The emotions have their own chemistry and sometimes some medication can help with emotional problems. Sometimes even because something is missing, like the insulin that a diabetic requires, and then maybe all you have to do is provide some pill and it controls the diabetes. Now what one strives for in diabetics also is to help them to develop eating habits that make it unnecessary for them to take insulin or a related drug. Here too our role will be for you to not need any medication eventually and to still be able to avoid your difficulties.

2. For the time being, the drug will be a good crutch to enable you to go around until you learn, with the help of some psychotherapy, to do it without that medication.

Hospitalization

1. Right now you are feeling really uncomfortable with yourself, not safe with yourself, scared of the world around you. It would help you feel more secure if, for a while, you would not have the ordinary responsibilities and rather just be in the hospital being taken care of, until you feel all right again.

SUICIDE

Precipitating Factor or Situation

1. When did you start feeling this way? I mean exactly. Not just what month or what week, but which day?
2. Where were you when you first thought of suicide?
3. What had happened that day?

Content and Concreteness and Primitivity of Fantasies and Plans

1. Tell me exactly how you plan to kill yourself.
2. What exactly are you going to do?
3. Where?
4. When?
5. How?

Previous Attempts (or Plans) and Attending Circumstances

1. Have you ever felt that way before?
2. When was that?
3. What was going on in your life at that time?

Family History of Suicidality or Depression

1. Did anybody in your family ever attempt or commit suicide? Father? Mother? Aunts? Cousins? Siblings? Grandparents?
2. Are there depressed people in your family? Who?

If Acutely Suicidal, Abandon Therapeutic Neutrality, Etc.

1. You know, so many people have committed suicide who, it turned out later, could have had very successful and happy lives, but were too rash and ended it all.
2. It would be a terrible thing if you were to really hurt yourself irreparably. There are so many people who love you and would be devastated if that happened. In fact, I think we want to make some plans for your own self-protection. I would like you to live with . . . until you are feeling much better.
3. And I want you to feel free to call me any time you really feel unhappy or preoccupied with suicide.
4. I also want to be able to call your spouse (parents, children, etc.) right now, while you are here with me, and tell them how you are feeling and that you might need some help and support and understanding from them.

Note: It may be helpful at this point to also engage in some cathartic interpretations.

5. I wonder whom you are really angry at that you have now turned that anger against yourself and want to even kill yourself—because that is what it really amounts to. You have a great deal of rage in you. Right now, you have rage at . . . and before you used to have a great deal of rage at your mother (father, sibling). Because you have a very strict conscience, you don't permit yourself to experience or express this anger and instead you turn it against yourself.

Note: Keep in mind all the variables discussed under Depression and Acting Out.

Work With Tunnel Vision

1. You know, you are like somebody who looks through a cardboard tube, and can see only what one can see through such a tube. You can think of only *that particular* hurt or *that particular* failure or *that particular* loss and you just don't see any alternatives.
2. The fact is that there any many options open to you, even though you can't see that right now. You can do _____or _____.

Note: Point out all the different alternatives to suicide. Help patient to make other choices. This may best include significant others in the patient's life.

Bargain for a Delay

1. Unfortunately, I can't keep you from committing suicide anyway. Nobody can. But it's also true that I won't be able to do anything about it a week from today, or two weeks from now, or next month . . . so why not give it a chance and work with me for now and if all goes well, you may feel much better and if not, you still have your options.

Work With Factors Pertaining to Depression or Panic

See Chapters on Depression and Panic

Draw Significant Others Into the Situation: Community Resources

1. You know that there is a 24-hour Suicide Prevention Service. Here is the number and you can always call and talk to somebody or actually go over there and see someone. So there is no need for you to feel lonely and without any help, even if you can't reach me.

Drugs, Hospitalization

Note: Suicidal patients need drugs which can be immediately effective. While anti-depressants may be indicated, they usually take too long to be effective. Anxiolitic drugs (prescribed in amounts not large enough to be used in a suicide attempt) may be preferable.

If in doubt, hospitalize!

It is very useful for the therapist to know who the patient's internist or general practitioner is and establish some liaison, just in case an acute suicidal attempt is made. In this event, the medical person will be much better equipped than the therapist to deal with the life-threatening emergency. Generally, it is very useful for anybody engaged in the treatment of relatively severely disturbed people to have a close working relationship with a hospital so that the patient can be briefly hospitalized, if necessary, to tide him over a particular danger. Active working-through can be done in that protective setting. Of course, pharmacotherapy and, in very rare instances, ECT, may be indicated.

1. I'd like to give you a drug that will make you feel a little less miserable. It's not a miracle drug and we will still need to understand why you feel the way that you do. It may, however, take the edge off your misery and actually permit us to work better. As soon as we understand what is going on with you, you'll be able to stop taking the drug.

2. Re: Hospitalization

I think basically you are really scared and you feel overwhelmed and lonely. While this feeling is most acute, it might be best for you to spend a few days in the protection of a hospital. It's a place where you won't feel alone, you'll know that there is somebody you can talk to and also have some protection against your own erratic impulses.

ENABLING CONDITIONS FOR THE INTENSIVE BRIEF AND EMERGENCY PSYCHOTHERAPY OF PSYCHOTICS

A Reasonably Cooperative, Non-Assaultive Patient: Facilitating Communication

1. I'm afraid you must be feeling awfully uncomfortable, scared, because of all the new things you are experiencing and can't make sense out of. And then you must wonder where I fit into all of this. And you are probably scared of me too.
2. One part of you, however, has remained a very sensible person and you know that something strange is happening to you. I need that sensible part of you to trust me a little and to work with me and I think that together we can try and understand what is happening to you. While this feels new to you, I have seen many people with similar difficulties and have been able to help with it. If we understand what is disturbing you, it will help to make it stop.
3. So why don't you tell me what's going on, how long it has been going on, what it is that you hear or see or think that is disturbing to you. Just give me some idea of what is going on. I know that it's difficult for you to talk, and in part that's because you feel scared and because these experiences of yours feel so odd and you don't understand them.
4. Tell me when it all started. What was the first thing that you noticed?
5. You know, the things that you are experiencing do have a rational meaning. We just have to find out the key to it. It probably feels a little bit like a dream, and we can certainly understand dreams.

At Least One Stable Relationship in the Patient's Life

1. I want to know who is closest to you. I would like to take that person into our confidence and tell them that you are extremely upset and are having all kinds of disturbing experiences, because I want somebody around who understands you to a certain extent and can help you, if necessary, when you are not seeing me.
2. I also want you to know about the medication that I am going to give you and just in case you are confused sometimes, it will be better if I can give this medication to this person you are close to. In fact, I would like him or her to come in or perhaps we can even call them right now and explain things. If not, I do want to see them next time and put them in the picture.
3. If you have a family whom you feel you are on pretty good terms with, you can ask them to come in next time.

A Close Relationship With a Nearby Hospital

1. If for some reason you should feel really desperate and disturbed, you might feel better in the hospital. A certain amount of protection might just make you feel

easier about it all. If possible, I would be glad to see you there too and help understand what is going on with you and then again when you come out and if we need to, further tie things together.

2. In the hospital, we can also try different medications and see which one helps you the most.

Optimally, A Family Network

1. I would want the family to visit you. We also can have a combined meeting with the family in the hospital and try to understand things and try to clear things up, particularly if you have trouble with somebody in the family.

Availability of an Auxiliary Therapist

1. You know, sometimes I might not be available or you might, in fact, develop some anger towards me or some other uncomfortable feelings. For that reason, you might not feel like talking to me. For that reason, you have the chance to talk to Dr. X or Miss Y (at the agency, the clinic, or some other office).

Awareness of Family and Community Resources: The "Y," "OVR", etc.

1. You know, you lead a very lonely life, which has much to do with your being upset. I want you to know that there is a "Y" not far from where you live, and it's a place where you can do something athletic as well as take some courses or watch TV with other people. There is also lots of other help available, aside from a 24-hour emergency line. Here is the number.

2. There are also social agencies you can turn to and they have experienced social workers on their staff who can help to understand what is going on with you and maybe see to it that you get to a rehabilitation center, where you can have structured work and see some other people in a controlled environment, which might make you feel better. You should know that you are eligible for medicare or other social insurance. A *social worker* would best be able to tell you just what. And if you are uncomfortable living alone, we may be able to find you what we call a *half-way house*, because it is half-way betweeen living home on one's own and living in the hospital, and you would have company there and a structured day and some experienced people to help you if you should not feel well.

Hot Lines and Emergency Centers

1. I certainly want you to know about this 24-hour *hot-line* and the emergency service. Here are the numbers. And if you lose this, you can find it in the front cover of the phone book and you can call them night or day.

Access to an Alarm System: Do Not Be a Hero

Note: See recommendations in BEP Handbook. To the tense patients you may also say the following:

1. You can say anything you want here, including whatever disturbing notions you have or any thoughts you might have about me. Only it has to remain just on a talking level.
2. And you have to be able to sit still in the chair and not pace around. Maybe you'll actually feel safer if we sit out in the hall or somewhere where other people are around also, since you may feel uncomfortable with me alone.

A Suitable Housing Situation

1. Where you are living now makes things more difficult for you. Being with the family is difficult for anybody and, in this case father (mother, brother, sister), especially rubs you the wrong way and it will be much easier to do something about your problems if you aren't exposed to the constant tension and irritation in the family. So we'll have to give some thought to where else you might live and maybe have a social worker or a social agency help to work that out.
2. Or perhaps there are *relatives* with whom you could stay or friends you would feel comfortable with, some place where you would feel better than you would if you remain with your family or spouse, because that's where the tension is. And then we can deal much better with what ails you, so that eventually you can go back if you want to.
3. And to be sure, here is some medication which will help you feel better.

Drug Therapy in Combination with Psychotherapy

1. This medication should make you feel better and will actually make you feel less panicky, less depressed, less scared of your disturbing experiences. In fact, it might do away with the things that you see and hear.
2. Now, it may have some side effects. You may get a dry mouth or you might feel a little woozy, slightly "out of it," in which case we can decrease the amount of medication. If you have more marked side effects, stop taking the medication and call me or your internist or go to the nearest emergency room. But to start with, it will make you feel less scared and more comfortable.
3. So you don't get mixed up, I'm going to give these pills to your spouse (father, mother, sister, brother) and ask them to hand it out to you, so that somebody can keep track.

ACUTE PSYCHOTIC STATES

Establish Contact

1. You must feel awfully scared and perplexed with all the new experiences you are having.
2. If you'll tell me just what your voices are saying and what you're seeing, we can try and make sense out of it. I may be able to help you to understand them, since it's a frightening new experience for you.
3. *What* exactly are the voices saying?
4. *Whose voice* do you think it is? It sounds like the voice of your conscience. Or maybe that's something that your father or mother said to you, once upon a time?
5. It sounds like you might be angry and think that these people know how angry you feel.
6. You must feel awfully bad about yourself to have you hear these things, which I think are your own opinion of yourself.
7. I wonder when all this started. Let's see if we can make some sense out of it. It seems to me that you started thinking that you were [e.g., a jazz star right after your girlfriend kicked you out] *or* [you started thinking you were rich and famous right after you lost your job]. You know, it sounds to me like that made you feel so small that you started thinking of making yourself that big!
8. It seems to me that you started thinking the FBI or the CIA were after you soon after you got angry at your mother (boss, whomever) and it sounds very much like your own conscience is pursuing you and making you feel that you are that bad, that dangerous a person. You are the one who feels that you are a bad person, a criminal, and we have to try and understand why you feel that way about yourself, why you have such a nasty view of yourself and when we understand it, then the FBI will stop bothering you.
9. You have a great deal of anger in you because . . . That's why you feel that everybody else has it in for you.

Establish Continuity

1. You know, one part of you knows that the things that trouble you are *not just there accidentally*. Why should it have started on one particular day? One particular week? There must have been a reason for it. We have to find out what that reason is.
2. I wonder if there was a time early in your life when you felt bad about yourself, thought little of yourself, thought that you were a bad person. You think that you are so bad now that you ought to be able to feel like Christ, to forgive everybody, so that you can also forgive your own anger.

3. You feel so lonely that you *wish* someone might be making noises upstairs, or would take the trouble to look at you through a telescope and watch you all the time. You were just terribly upset to be left alone when your daughter (son, etc.) moved away and I think that is when your problems started to escalate.

Reassure by Interpretation and Understanding

1. If we can understand *why* you feel the way that you do, and *why* you hear and see things the way you do, they will go away. Together, we'll work on it until we can understand things.
2. You know, every time you point out that the radiator next to my chair is turning red, you are also turning red with anger, getting "hot" under the collar.

Structure the Patient's Life

1. You have so much time on your hands that it's like daydreaming. You have filled your fantasy life with voices and seeing things. If you'll get busier, that alone will help to deal with it. I suggest that a rehabilitation workshop might help, where you can find some constructive work and some people to talk to, and you would not be that lonely. It would get you out of bed in the morning. It gives you a chance to not be totally preoccupied with yourself and it gets you accustomed to talking to other people, to be able to tolerate them, first in small doses and then in larger doses. That's what rehab workshops are for.

Be Available

1. If you are in a real panic or in real trouble and you want to call me, it's perfectly all right. I won't always be sitting by the phone, so you can't count on me answering immediately, but at the very least, I'll get the message and I'll call you back.
2. Also, I want you to know that there is the Hotline (give patient the number), where you can always find someone to talk to, or you can even go over to the clinic so that you don't need to feel that you are all alone without any other help.

Involve Significant Others

1. Also, it's better if you level with your spouse (father, mother, brother, friend), and tell them what is disturbing you these days. If they can't understand or it is too upsetting to them, bring them in here and we can all discuss it together. But it will be better for you to be able to talk to somebody who knows something about what ails you so you do not feel entirely on your own.

Splinting

1. Right now, it's difficult for you to carry these many courses. It's like a balancing act and you're constantly scared that you're going to drop something. I think if

you will simplify your load, you'll find yourself less strained and that, by itself, will decrease the things that trouble you.

2. At the moment, you don't have very much energy, even for doing the daily things you have to do, particularly with the children making their demands. So I suggest that you see a social worker and arrange for a homemaker to help and anything else that will decrease the burden until we and time itself help heal the wounds that bother you right now.

Therapist as Auxiliary Ego

1. You know, when one person tells you that you're drunk, you can disregard it. When two people tell you, you might still not pay attention. But when three tell you the same thing, you had better start taking it easy.

Drugs

1. These drugs will help particularly right for this moment. I don't mean to keep you on drugs forever, but it's a little bit like dislocating an arm and getting splints on it, until it heals again, maybe with the help of heat, etc. So, similarly, taking these drugs has a "splinting" function for your personality and will make you less scared, less angry, less restless, and meanwhile, we can try and understand what makes you feel that way and try and deal with the real causes and when we have done that successfully, it will be time to stop the drugs again.

Brief Hospitalization

1. I think you felt scared of your own impulses, of yourself. You have a feeling you don't know what you might do, and that scares you. It will help you if you can spend a little while in the hospital, where you can feel protected against yourself, against your own impulses. And then when we have taken the edge off things, and you feel more comfortable with yourself, you can leave again. It's just a temporary measure, primarily to make you feel more comfortable and less threatened.

PHYSICAL ILLNESS OR SURGERY

Explore the Patient's Concept of the Illness or Impending Surgery

1. Tell me exactly what ails you. Can you draw me a picture of where your problem is? An ulcer? A diverticulum? The cervix?
2. Can you draw me a picture of the whole area? Your ideas about the organs involved are not exactly on target. Let's discuss it.
3. When was the problem first discovered?
4. What did you think when you were told?
5. If they tell you that you will need surgery, tell me what you would expect to happen? The night before? When they take you to the operating room? After the operation?
6. You know, you will probably receive sedation the night before. I guess the major nuisance might be when you check into the hospital because probably about five people will come around asking you the same questions—the medical student, the intern, the resident, your regular doctor, then probably at least one nurse, one nurse practitioner, probably two or three people will come and try to get blood from your vein. Chances are one will come back because he or she has forgotten something and just when you think it would be nice to fall asleep, somebody will come maybe and shave you so that the field for the operation should be entirely clean.
7. Above all, when you go into the hospital, you lose your freedom. Everybody is your boss, including student nurses. And sometimes you wonder if they know what they are doing.
8. One of the people who should come around and whom you have a right to ask to come around is the anesthetist. You want to know what kind of anesthesia to expect, and you should understand precisely how it works. If it is a spinal anesthesia, you will probably stay more or less awake, just very much sedated. As if you are in a half-sleep.
9. After the operation you will go to the recovery room, where they have excellent nurses who will keep a very close watch on you. If you had a spinal, the most disturbing thing will be that you can't move your feet, your toes or legs, until half an hour or more, when you can first wiggle your toes. It's an alarming feeling. But once you can wiggle your toes, they will push you back into your private room.
10. All the tubes one gets in one's mouth or nose or into the veins looks a lot worse than they really are. Even something stuck down into the esophagus, the tube that leads food into the stomach, is something that one gets very quickly accustomed to. Just the way you don't feel gloves a while after you have put them on. And the tubes in the veins, after a while they hang the bottle from a stand and you can even go walking with it. And after a while you'll forget about that too.

11. If something concerns you, *ask*. If you are afraid of pain after the operation, make sure that your doctor leaves an order which we call PRN, when necessary—so that they don't have to start searching for an intern when you have a pain and want a pain killer or a sleeping pill.

Personal Meaning and Role of the Illness

1. I wonder how you see yourself *after* the surgery and what your worst fears are? Where do you get these notions from? Who else had something like that in the family? Among your acquaintances?

Educate the Patient

1. Let's discuss all the implications, the whole picture—what it means, what it doesn't mean.

Establish Contact with Treating Physician

1. If necessary, I'll talk to your doctor and see exactly what he has to say or what he has in mind and then I'll help and translate it for you and also tell him of your concerns. You know that surgeons especially aren't great on talking—they feel their job is just the surgery. But I'll impress him with the fact that patients who know what it is about don't have unnecessary anxiety and recover much better than others who don't know. So let's make that clear to him.

Explore the Meaning of Anesthesia

1. You know, many people still have the notion of anesthesia that goes back to when they or their kids had their tonsils out under ether. It felt like choking and fiery and when one came to, one frequently had to throw up and was feeling perfectly awful. But that's not the way it is anymore. You get what is called pre-sedation either my mouth or by injection, which makes you peaceful. The so-called inhalation anesthesias are often just used as a little extra, while you might just get intravenous valium or sodium amytal, or maybe a spinal in addition.
2. Anesthesia has developed into a superb science, where several people constantly watch you and do what is necessary to make it as comfortable and safe as possible.

Specific Notions and Fears of Death

1. Just what is it exactly that you fear the most? Being crippled? Dying? Having terrible pains?
2. What is your fantasy of what is going to happen to you?
3. What nightmarish thoughts have you had about it?
4. What's the worst that you expect?

Specific Types of Illness and Surgery

1. Different types of operations awaken different kinds of anxieties. For example: You need an intestinal operation and the doctors will have to make a "temporary" colostomy, which is an opening in your abdominal wall, a sort of artificial anus, I think that might upset you because it seems like such a dirty thing to do and you are afraid you won't be able to control your feces. Actually I want you to know that something like a sphincter, a closing-off muscle is being built in, and these days it is often done in such a way that it is so small and comfortable that I have known attractive young women to wear bikinis, despite the fact that they have had a colostomy—and live happily afterwards for many decades.

   Note: Re Prostatectomy, hysterectomy, ovarectomy

2. Of course, anything that involves the *sexual* apparatus—(like your prostate, uterus, ovaries, etc.)—threatens one's masculinity or femininity. As a woman facing a hysterectomy, you may understandably fear not being able to experience any sexual desire or pleasure anymore. That is absolutely not so.

RE: Prostate Surgery

3. *Men* most usually are afraid that a prostate operation will make them impotent. Especially if it's merely transurethral that is exceedingly unlikely and it happens only occasionally. Even if the operation has to be suprapubic (explain to patient briefly what is involved), that doesn't necessarily mean impotence. In a large percentage of cases, the ability for an erection and the desire for sexual activity will remain entirely intact. One thing that does happen with these operations is that very often ejaculations are retrograde—that is, the ejaculation goes into the bladder rather than outside, but otherwise the sensations remain the same. I wonder what you are particularly concerned about?

4. You know that *women* who have had their uterus and ovaries removed do not lose either their sexual desire or their ability to have intercourse, because the vagina is left intact.

5. Breast surgery, of course, is a particularly upsetting experience, especially when the breast has to be removed, but you know that there are a variety of techniques now in plastic surgery that can replace the lost breast. It's something that you will want to discuss carefully with your surgeon.

Malignancies

1. Cancer is the big scare word. What one has to know about it is that malignancies, cancers, and their relatives are of *widely different nature* and luckily, many of them can be cured these days or treated in such a way that they still give one a chance for a long life expectancy.

2. We have to know precisely what ails you and what can then be done about it, and that will depend upon the types of cells found and whether it is all localized

or has spread. If necessary, there is the possibility of chemotherapy, as well as radiation. Neither of these is fun. While they are going on, they are likely to make you feel quite sick and nauseous, which the doctors will try to control.

3. But it is important that we discuss right now all your notions of what your worst fears are. You may also want to talk to others who had such surgery for this condition, but it might be best to wait and see whether there is a real problem. There may not be. And if there is, you might profit from talking to a small group of people with similar problems.

4. Meanwhile, I want *precisely your idea* of how you think the cancer might look and how it works and how it comes about and what your notions and fears are. Did you have any dreams lately?

Heart Disease

1. The heart plays a large, symbolic role—as the center of life—so anything that ails the heart frightens one particularly. I wonder if you can draw me a picture of the heart and tell me how you think it works and what might be wrong with yours. Now let's discuss it in detail.

2. The heart is really just a pump and one side of the pump pushes blood out into the circulatory system, and the other one draws it in. Now it does not work efficiently if the valves aren't tight and so what your doctors want to do is something like priming a pump—tighten the valve again so that it should work more efficiently.

    In the case of angina or in any narrowing of the blood vessels (because cholesterol deposits have made them narrower), they may want to do a by-pass. This means that they will close off some troublesome artery, and put in a new piece taken from the leg. In essence, they are just doing a "shunting" of the bloodstream, so that you should have an open passage rather than a partially closed one (which also could shoot flakes of cholesterol or calcium into other parts of the body), which could be very troublesome.

3. You will want to ask your cardiologist and your surgeon any questions that come to your mind. They probably even have some booklets that tell a good deal about this and then, if necessary, you and I can discuss it further. What is it that you fear the most?

4. I wonder just what your *fears of dying* are.

5. How do you imagine dying and what do you think happens after you die?

CATASTROPHIC LIFE EVENTS

Catharsis

1. Tell me exactly what happened and don't try to be a hero. After all, I want to know what scared you, what you felt, what you dreamt, and just let it all hang out. This is not a place to control yourself.

Specific Meaning of Event

1. What's important is for you to tell me exactly how you feel.
2. How did you really feel about the burglary (rape, mugging, etc.) and do you feel that you should have behaved differently?
3. Do you feel that what happened is in any way your fault?
4. What did you feel at the time that it happened?
5. What were your worst concerns?
6. Whom are you most afraid to tell about it?
7. You know, different people will experience the same thing in quite different ways. I want to know just exactly what this unfortunate event means to you, and what troubles you expect from it.

Exploration of "Liability" and Guilt

1. It's very important that you tell me what dreams you have had since the event so that we can understand just what your unconscious notions are of what happened, what your conscience says about it, whom you are angry at, what similar feelings in the past your feelings now resemble.

Prevention of Chronic Sequaelae

1. If you don't get it all out of your system now, it will kick up trouble later. Once when there was a tremendous fire in a Boston nightclub, those survivors who tried to keep a stiff upper lip later often developed ulcers and other disorders, as if the upset and the emotions which didn't come out in words had to come out in some physical illness or a later depression, so it's important that you tell me all about it.

Specific Responses to Job Loss and Retirement

1. Losing one's job, or being forced to retire, regardless of what one may know intellectually, feels like one just got a kick in the pants and doesn't want it. And it makes you feel worthless, disappointed, deceived, angry, hopeless, quite aside

from financial losses. One also feels that one has lost one's role, one's usefulness, one's meaning in life.

2. And it's very important that you plan what to do and have a very regular regimen and a useful one, not just playing cards, because we all need meaning in our lives, and it's important that we find exactly what will make you feel useful and give you very specific things to do for a structured day.

Specific Responses to Loss Through Death: Bereavement

1. Whenever someone loses someone through death, it feels like a tremendous loss and one feels gypped and left behind and deceived, and one feels angry, irrational as it sounds, at the fact that the other person has left one.
2. We will want to discuss all of your feelings, even those which you don't even permit yourself to have. It's only normal to have these feelings. In fact, what happened to you even before he or she died is that you anticipated the death— what might be called *preliminary mourning*—so that you really started mourning quite some time before.

Specific Responses to Mugging and Burglary

1. All burglaries, all muggings, feel like a personal intrusion. We identify with our apartment, our house, and somebody breaking in feels like a personal bodily violation, and certainly mugging is a frightening experience where one feels helpless and demeaned. Especially for men, that is often difficult to bear because it interferes with their masculine self-esteem, while women often feel all the more helpless and they may even interpret the mugging not involving any sexual threat as something of a symbolic rape.
2. We will want to explore all the meanings this has had for you, to avoid any later repercussions.

Specific Responses to Rape

1. There is an old fairy tale to the effect that the woman is somehow responsible for "having let herself be raped." Some believe that she provoked it by her behavior or by being careless as to where she went, or to whose apartment she went. The fact is that rape is not even really a sexual crime. *It is a crime of violence.* The man has sadistic notions, probably because he feels quite inferior himself, and tries to assert his masculinity by a sadistic, violent attack. *The rape itself frequently makes no sense*, since senile old ladies have at times been raped, as well as children and others of all ages.
2. *Numb Stage*
Right now, you are just feeling numb and are remembering how paralyzed you felt at first and just wanted to survive. Now you are probably blaming yourself for not having fought more actively, which indeed might just have gotten you killed.

41

Denial

3. I can't believe that you are as "cool" right now about it as you seem to be, and I suspect that you are just trying to shove it under the rug, whereas it will only kick up trouble later on. So it's really better that we have it all out because if you don't, later on you may really recoil from yourself. Sometimes women become socially withdrawn because they are ashamed and scared and then also mourn their loss of self-esteem.

Shame

4. I don't think you should be afraid to tell your husband. You're behaving as if it were your fault, and it is his business to understand and support you, not to be critical. If he is critical, it is because he doesn't understand what is involved and he should come around so all three of us can discuss it.

5. Of course, you may not want to let people on the job know or others in the neighborhood, since sometimes it does indeed arouse some morbid feelings, though it's certainly all right to discuss it with your close friends.

6. As you know, there are *specific rape counseling centers,* if you would feel more comfortable with a woman who has had a great deal of experience with this particular problem.

Specific Responses to Accidents

1. At first, you simply feel stunned. There is a sudden interruption of your life from simply going along, doing one thing after another, to suddenly being in this accident which has disrupted your whole life pattern. This has had a devastating effect. You feel totally disoriented, as if you were spinning on a merry-go-round, not knowing where you are.

2. You are trying to make sense out of the experience, reliving it again in your mind, to see what you would have done differently, trying to absorb exactly what happened to you.

3. I guess maybe you even blame yourself for having done certain things and not others, and you are still attempting to make sense out of what happened to you.

4. I guess you even feel the way you did at other times in your life, when something very upsetting happened to you.

Specific Response to Ecological Threats

1. When there is an earthquake, one really feels that one can't trust anything, one can't even trust Mother Earth to behave quietly. One is literally shaken to one's foundations. One has a fear that everything will fall in on oneself.

2. There is indeed a danger of accidental nuclear catastrophies, but if you're constantly worrying about it, it's a little bit like the person I knew who was constantly afraid that the ceiling might fall in. I couldn't say that it was impossible, but luckily it was very unlikely, and luckily so far nuclear catastrophies are relatively unlikely. There is always danger in life but one will be unable to function at all if all one does is to focus on what *might* happen. There must be a particular personal reason why you feel that a catastrophe might occur practically all the time.

PHOBIAS (AND ANXIETY HYSTERIAS)

General Questions

1. Tell me exactly when and where you first became anxious.
2. What exactly is it that you fear will happen?
3. Can you describe it more accurately?
4. When did it first occur?
5. What year? What month? What day?
6. Where were you?
7. What were you doing?
8. What was going on in your life then?
9. What did you imagine would happen to you when you got scared?
10. What fears did you have as a child?
11. What nightmares did you have?
12. Did you have any recurrent dreams?
13. What did you dream last night?
14. Tell me a little bit about your parents (brother, sister, other people in your life).
15. Where did you live?
16. How did you live?
17. Did you have a room of your own?
18. Where was it?
19. With whom did you share it?
20. Aside from what you have already told me, what else bothers you?
21. Who else in your family has similar fears?
22. What medical illnesses have you had?
23. What illnesses do you have at present?
24. What kind of medication are you taking for it?
25. Are you taking any kind of street drugs?

Specific Dynamics of the Different Phobias

1. Let's see if we can understand a little bit of what is going on with you. Whenever you do . . . you feel anxious. That's very similar to . . . in your childhood or what goes on in your dreams . . .
2. What do you think this might mean?
3. Well, I think that all these conditions have in common the fact that . . .
4. It seems that whenever you . . . ., you get anxious. I will give you some medication that will decrease the anxiety a little. It doesn't perform miracles and it's really just a temporary help, but with the help of the pills, you might soon be able to face your fears a little bit at a time. If you're afraid of driving, you might try to drive around the block just once.

5. If you're afraid of walking on the street, try to only cross the street.
6. If you have a fear of dogs, play first with a toy dog and then a puppy dog.
7. If even this seems like too much, you might first try to imagine doing these things and then when you don't feel too anxious imagining it, you can take the next step.
8. It is important that you face a little bit of what you are afraid of and what you did and what you felt. That way we can learn more about what troubles you and why and can get further along with helping you to conquer your fear.
9. In part, what's going to happen is that you will be able to unlearn and relearn things which you learned the wrong way. And while you know that your fears are absurd, you can't help having them anyway.
10. Whenever you are about to feel anxious, I want you to think about what we have learned, maybe even say it out loud to yourself. Think about the basic common factors. The more often you can do that, the better you will unlearn your anxieties.

Example of a Specific Phobia: Agoraphobia

1. What are you afraid might happen to you?
2. Are you afraid of fainting?
3. What are you afraid will happen after you faint?
4. Are there conditions under which you are *not* afraid to walk across the street? To walk by yourself?
5. What do you think people might do to you?
6. When you were a kid, were you afraid of going to school?
7. Did your mother have to go with you when you were in kindergarten and sit there for quite some time?
8. What were you afraid of then?
9. Were you afraid of what might happen to you or your mother?
10. How did your mother treat you when you were a kid?
11. Was she very anxious when she tried to protect you against everything?
12. Would you say that she was overly close? Did that bother you?

Specific Phobias as Part of a Family and Cultural Context

1. Does anybody in your family have similar fears? Similar ways of behaving?
2. You know, sometimes one simply "learns" these fears—from parents, etc. In some cultures, it is customary to stay close to the parents and then whenever one has to move away, one feels scared. Is that the way it goes in your family?

Overdetermined Individual Pathogenesis of Phobias

1. Lots of people have phobias. What we want to understand is yours specifically and what makes you anxious under what particular circumstances, in distinction to anybody else who may have similar fears. We want to understand the *precise meaning* of your particular fears.

2. Of course it doesn't have to be reasonable. I'm a specialist for the unreasonable, so tell me exactly what you are afraid of.

Ask the Patient to Face the Phobic Situation and Report Back

1. Now that we understand a little bit of what goes on with you, it's important that you try and bear a little bit of the anxiety and, say, drive a mile or take the subway for one stop or anything else you can manage and then see how you feel. Come back and tell me all about your feelings. In that way, we will have new insights, we learn more about what's going on in you and then we can take it from there.

Work Through Insights Obtained in the Actual Phobic Situation

1. Then we can "work through" exactly what scares you and in that way go a step further.

Drugs for Symptomatic Relief of Some Phobias

1. If it's really terrible for you, I am quite willing to give you some drugs which may make it a bit more bearable while we still learn something from what you experience.
2. You know, the drugs themselves are not going to perform any miracles, but they may serve as a "splint," in the way that we sometimes splint a dislocated arm, making it possible for you to do something that you otherwise would be unable to do, which may have its practical advantages, but, above all, will be grist for our mill.

Counter-Phobic Symbols and Defenses

1. I understand that if you can have your rabbit's foot or anything else that sometimes makes you feel better and less scared. We will have to understand what role this particular thing plays for you, and then that will help you with your anxieties.

Migratory Phobias

1. Sometimes it is as if one could change from being scared of one thing to being scared of another, hardly without pausing. That's because you have a very general anxiety and it attaches itself to practically anything. So we'll want to understand that general anxiety and how it attaches itself first to one thing and then to another.
2. We want to understand why your general anxiety migrates through your whole body. Because if you are really constantly overwhelmed, we may indeed want to give you some drugs or you might feel better having a few days in the hospital, until you feel less tortured by all this.

PANIC

Note: In an endrogenous panic, the task of the therapist is to establish continuity by finding out the unconscious precipitating factors for the panic.

General Questions

Endrogenous Panic

1. It feels very peculiar, I know, to be panicky, without even knowing exactly what is scaring you, to just have this great feeling of impending disaster—your heart beats faster, you breathe faster, you are afraid that you will faint.
2. We will try and get at what is causing this, because there are no miracles. Sometimes something unconscious, something that we are unaware of, can bother us and make the heart beat faster or any of the other things that you are experiencing. Whatever is going on with you might also come out in your dreams, but doesn't quite emerge when you are awake, and we have to find out what that is. So let's see.
3. When did you last feel panicky?
4. Anytime before that?
5. When was the first time you ever felt panicky?
6. Where were you?
7. What had happened that day?
8. That week?
9. What was going on in your life at that time?

Exogenous Panic

1. Of course, having such a dreadful experience would make anyone feel terribly scared. Maybe it brings up other things and other times when you were dreadfully scared, when it was perfectly natural to feel that way. Something in your present life situation is bringing up other things from the past that scared you.

The "Mixed" Panic

1. Sometimes taking street drugs like PCP, pot, speed, downers and all that, can make one feel extremely scared. If that's what you did, we will still want to understand your fears, but the drugs are the main reason that you feel panicky right now. We also want to explore why it was necessary for you to take the drugs.
2. As the drug wears off, I expect you to feel better.

Establish the Unconscious Cause of the Endogenous Panic

1. Sometimes an anniversary of a painful event may make one feel panicky without one knowing that that is the reason. Is that the case with you?
2. Being separated from somebody one is extremely close to, as in the case of a child going away to camp, may produce a panic.
3. If you feel that you have done something bad, and even though you may reasonably know that it is not (so) awful, your conscience may bite you and that might cause a panic.
4. If you suddenly feel like you're absolutely no good, totally worthless, that changes your whole outlook on life, and can cause a panic.
5. At times, anxiety makes one feel as if one were not real, or the world around one is not real, and in turn, that may further make one feel extremely anxious. Do you feel as if you are on the outside looking in, and not being quite connected? Sometimes just the overbreathing that occurs when one is anxious may make one feel "out of it."
6. Sometimes one may have the eerie feeling of having already experienced something, having already seen it. Then one feels "out of it," odd.
7. Of course, overwhelming experiences may make one panicky. Soldiers who have experienced terrible traumas may be in a panic. If you were exposed to a terrifying experience, it's only reasonable that you would feel panicky.

Continuity Between Immediate Panic, Precipitating Factors and Life History

Note: In both the exogenous and the endogenous panic, it is important to understand what the unconscious meanings hold for the patient.

1. What scares you now seems to have come from out of the blue. As a matter of fact, though, if you look at what's going on in your life, it's the same thing that scared you several times in your early life . . . You're simply not aware of the fact that every time somebody threatens to leave (e.g., earlier threat of your parent's divorce; the time they left you home when they went on a trip, your going away to school, the time your girlfriend left you, etc.) you had these same feelings, i.e., feelings of unreality, of light-headedness, of a fear of impending doom and destruction, the experience of nightmares in which you feel helpless, out of control, attacked.
2. It's important for us to realize that there are these common denominators in what ails you and that it can be understood and unlearned.

Intellectual Explanation as Part of Establishing Continuity

1. You know, I'm going to try and explain to you what I think is troubling you. I know it will be hard for you to see this as meaningful. All I wish to do, however, at present, is to give you a little inkling that what ails you can be understood at least

intellectually—and that may make you feel better because at least you will have some kind of handle on it.

Exogenous Panic: Unconscious Meaning of External Event

Note: With the exogenous panic, what we have to find out from the patient is what irrational factors may add to the rational ones of being scared. Usually the irrational ones are worse; what it means to the patient, rather than the actual facts per se.

1. You know, if the same thing had happened to ten other people, they would have reacted entirely differently from you. Incidentally, some may have reacted with a great deal of panic, and some with none at all. This illustrates that it isn't necessarily what actually happened, but what the happening *means to you* that determines how you reacted, including the panic that you have experienced.

Endogenous Panic as Part of Incipient Psychosis

1. If, all of a sudden you aren't sure who you are, where you are, you hear strange voices—of course that will make you feel suddenly disconnected from the world. It's a terrifying feeling to be in your own world and not have other people hear and see and feel the things that you do. It's understandable that you feel panicky.

Be Completely Available to the Patient

1. In a severe panic, of course one feels like a drowning child. One wants to hold on to something, anything, anybody. While you are feeling this way, I'll want to be as available to you as possible. You can call me during the night, you can call the hotline.
2. I'm willing to do whatever I can for you, until you are feeling better.

Interpret Denial

1. To be panicky is human and to deny it and feel you have to be a hero and pretend that nothing can affect you is not helpful.

Catharsis and Mediate Catharsis

1. If you can let out your feelings here and simply tell me how terrified you felt, it would help.
2. I would have certainly been scared out of my skin if that sort of thing had happened to me.
3. I have experienced anxiety myself, so I want you to feel entirely free to tell me everything that you are feeling and thinking.

FEELINGS OF UNREALITY OF THE SELF AND OF THE WORLD

Co-Existence of Feelings of Unreality of the Self and of the World

1. Everyone of us sometimes feels as if we are on the outside looking in, and it's a strange feeling. It makes you feel eerie, not quite with it. If it gets bad, it could be like feeling one is behind a glass wall or enclosed in plastic and not really in touch with other people.
2. Sometimes it's about oneself and sometimes one feels that the world around one doesn't look real, but rather eerie, strange. One feels "out of it."

A Continuum of Pathology

1. Many people experience these feelings of unreality when they suffer from stage fright. If you have ever been in a drama group, you might know that when you have to take a few steps or look out into the crowd, you might suddenly feel as if it is a very difficult job just to move your feet. You suddenly become aware of walking when you never were before.
2. If you have ever had to give a toast at dinner, or to give an important speech, you might have suddenly felt as if everyone were staring at you. Your heart begins to beat faster, and you feel strange, not quite "with it." Sometimes people appear farther away than they really are. Such feelings are quite uncomfortable.
3. Some people have these sensations when they are engaged in sex. Suddenly they hear all the street noises and everything else and feel themselves to be far removed and not really "with it."
4. These feelings may emerge sometimes because one feels scared, and one starts observing oneself and everything around one, to a greater degree than one would ordinarily. The moment that that happens you sort of split part of yourself off and observe the rest of you and it doesn't feel natural.
5. You know, there's an old story that when a centipede starts to worry about which leg to move next, he is paralyzed and that's the sort of thing that apparently happens to you sometimes.
6. Some people have feelings of unreality, as we sometimes call it, just as the result of overbreathing. If you breathe too fast in and out, you blow off a great deal of carbon dioxide, and we say that your blood pressure becomes more alkaline and that alone can give one a feeling of strangeness. Parts of your fingers might start tingling, your arm might feel heavy, you might feel a little dizzy and disoriented.
7. You know, when the muscles of the neck get stiff, one can get to feel as if he were on a merry-go-round, because these muscles have something to do with one's sense of equilibrium. At least if you can understand that such simple things as these can cause a feeling of unreality, it may be a bit easier to bear. We'll still have to find out why you get that scared.

8. We can probably decrease these feelings by simply giving you some kind of a mild tranquilizer, but that wouldn't be dealing with the situation as thoroughly as we want to. You don't want to have to be on tranquilizers all the time, although you can take one if you have a special situation coming up that you know will be very stressful. But otherwise, it's better if we just try and understand what it is all about.

States of Heightened and Changed Awareness of the Self and/or the Body

1. If you are accustomed to living very close to your family, then just leaving them might make you suddenly feel like part of you is missing. This can produce feelings of estrangement and fear of aloneness. You might suddenly feel that the world is unreal or that suddenly you are all by yourself.
2. Sometimes you might not feel that all of you is unreal, but rather just a part of you—your lips might feel dead or perhaps just one hand or an arm might feel strange, practically as if it didn't belong to you, certainly a very alarming feeling.
3. Most frequent is a disturbance in vision. Suddenly things will seem fuzzy or you might experience double vision. It's not hard to do when one feels anxious. I can show you. If you look just at my finger and then at the distance behind me, you might see my fingers as double. If that sort of thing occurs without your knowing why, it might make you feel pretty anxious.
4. Sometimes when one is in a strange city and walking down a street like Wall Street, with its very tall buildings and narrow streets, one might begin to feel awfully small and scared and even unreal. If you are far away from home, from all that is familiar, and that feeling hits you, you can feel you're all on your own, all by yourself, and that can produce a lot of anxiety.

Aggressive, Sexual, Exhibitionistic and Separation Aspects

1. Sometimes, when one doesn't approve of some feelings or wishes or impulses that one has, one behaves as if they did not belong to one but rather to someone else. At the same time, it can be very scary to have the thought that you want to hit somebody, or to walk around nude. It makes you feel strange about yourself.
2. One part of you has these ideas and wishes, which of course we will try to understand the reason for. The other part of you, however, is reasonable and alarmed about all this, and this can make you feel almost as if you were two people.
3. What we have to try to do therapeutically is to see that you get in touch with the unreasonable part of you and understand why you feel the way you do, and then these undesirable thoughts or wishes should go away.

Disturbances of the Sense of Self as Intra-Systemic Ego Disturbances

1. As mentioned, sometimes one part of oneself doesn't approve of what another part of the self is thinking, feeling or doing. That can easily create a feeling of one looking from the outside in, and feeling distant and unreal, which is very frightening.

50

Estrangement Related to Physical Factors

1. If one is scared, one often breathes too fast and blows off too much carbon dioxide. That makes the blood more alkaline and that fact alone can cause all kinds of trouble. It may cause spasms of the small muscles between the ribs and might give one the scary idea that it's a heart attack. Sometimes it can cause one to have a stiff neck. The powerful neck muscles have something to do with the sense of equilibrium and if they are cramped, one might have a sensation of dizziness, light headedness, and a feeling of being unreal.

Drug-Induced States of Unreality

1. Sometimes taking drugs can produce feelings of depersonalization. Many people, when they take tranquilizers, report that they suddenly feel "out of it," "spacy," and so I wonder if you have been taking anything that might have caused this kind of a reaction.

Déjà Vu and Déjà Reconnu Phenomena

1. Sometimes one has the eerie feeling of having already seen something, when you have good reason to know that you never have. We have fancy French terms, Déjà Vu and Déjà Reconnu, having already seen something or the feeling that you have already experienced something. Sometimes that happens simply because you have already anticipated in fantasy how something will look or what somebody will say. Then when it actually happens, it feels as if you had already lived through the situation.

General Therapeutic Considerations

1. You know, these days some people have these feelings of unreality when they are not accustomed to flying and they hop into a plane in New York and a few hours later are in Paris, and they might well at times feel, "My God, where am I?" "How come?" "What's going on?" And then just breathing a little faster and heavier will produce the tingling and some awkward feelings in the arm, maybe even in the chest, because there are little muscles between the ribs which are very responsive to overbreathing and they become tight and one might get scared that he is going to have a heart attack. We can fix those things. If you have a straw or a rolled up paper and make a little tube and breathe in normally and then breathe out through the tube or just before completely breathing out, then remove it and really let your breath out, keeping that up for two minutes or so, your breathing will become regular again and you'll stop having that feeling. Or you can breathe into a paper bag. The idea is that when you exhale, you exhale, you exhale more carbon dioxide than when you inhale, because when you inhale, you inhale a richer mixture of carbon dioxide and air, and the carbon dioxide will have a good effect on the eerie feeling and the tingling and all that.

Drug Management

1. For the time being, if nothing helps, it will pay to take a small amount of tranquilizers just to start learning that the feeling can be controlled, and then when you find out what makes you tick, it shouldn't be necessary to have the pills.